Contents

- **2** Introduction/The Romans
- **4** St. Albans 30 CE
- **6** St. Albans 50 CE
- **8** Boudica destroys St. Albans
- **10** St. Albans 150 CE
- **12** St. Albans 270 CE
- **14** The Roman Theatre
- **16** The Floral Mosaic
- **18** The Shell Mosaic
- **20** The Oceanus Mosaic
- **22** The Venus Figurine
- **24** Roman amphorae
- **26** The Town Wall
- **28** The Basilica and Forum
- **30** The Temple of Cybele
- **32** Roman St. Albans today

Symbols used in this guide

Outlines of Roman walls
(still visible)

Outlines of Roman walls
(no longer visible)

 Theatre

Roman points of interest
(still visible)

Temple

Roman points of interest
(no longer visible)

Verulamium Museum

Roman Theatre of Verulamium

Roman St. Albans looking north, 270 CE.

Introduction

St. Albans has a long and complex history, spanning over two thousand years. Today it is a thriving city dominated by St. Albans Cathedral. Arguably St. Albans is most well known for its extensive Roman history, including the devastating attack by Boudica. This guide explores the period from 30 CE to 270 CE. After this date the Roman Empire started a gradual decline and by 410 CE Britain was under constant attack by marauding Anglo-Saxons.

The guide brings to life how St. Albans could have looked in Roman times, with full-colour 3D maps all looking north *(unless specified otherwise)*, reconstructions of mosaics and artefacts. There are also detailed maps showing where each site or artefact is in present-day St. Albans.

This guide suggests the location of an amphitheatre, at the time of writing one has not been found, but most Roman towns in Britain had one.

Towns and cities
The Romans defined towns and cities differently to how we do in the present day. They had three main types of town:
- *A Colonia, which was a rough equivalent of a city.*
- *A Municipium, which was slightly less important than a colonia.*
- *A Civitas capital, which was a broad equivalent of a large market town.*

The Romans called pre-Roman towns 'oppida'.

The Romans

The city of Rome in central Italy was formed around 800 BCE and grew over the centuries into the Roman Empire, which covered most of Europe and northern Africa. It was a highly sophisticated and technologically advanced society, with a huge army, major roads and large cities.

Britain at that time was a mysterious place with fierce tribes and valuable metals, which became the focus of an attempted invasion in 55 BCE and 54 BCE by Julius Caesar.

Those invasions were repelled by local tribes and the Romans did not try again to invade Britain for almost 100 years.

By 43 CE the Emperor Claudius *(who needed the army's support)* decided to invade Britain, which was weakened by the death of King Cunobelin of the Trinovantes, who lived in Camulodunum *(Colchester)*. After attacking Colchester the Roman forces then moved west across England, including where present day St. Albans is located...

Visiting St. Albans

St. Albans lies about 25 miles (40km) north of London. There are two main museums which show Roman St. Albans in depth:
The Verulamium Museum in the Verulamium Park and the Roman Theatre of Verulamium Museum (a short distance from the Verulamium Museum). Remains of the Roman Town Wall and a Roman Hypocaust/Mosaic can also be seen in the Verulamium Park.

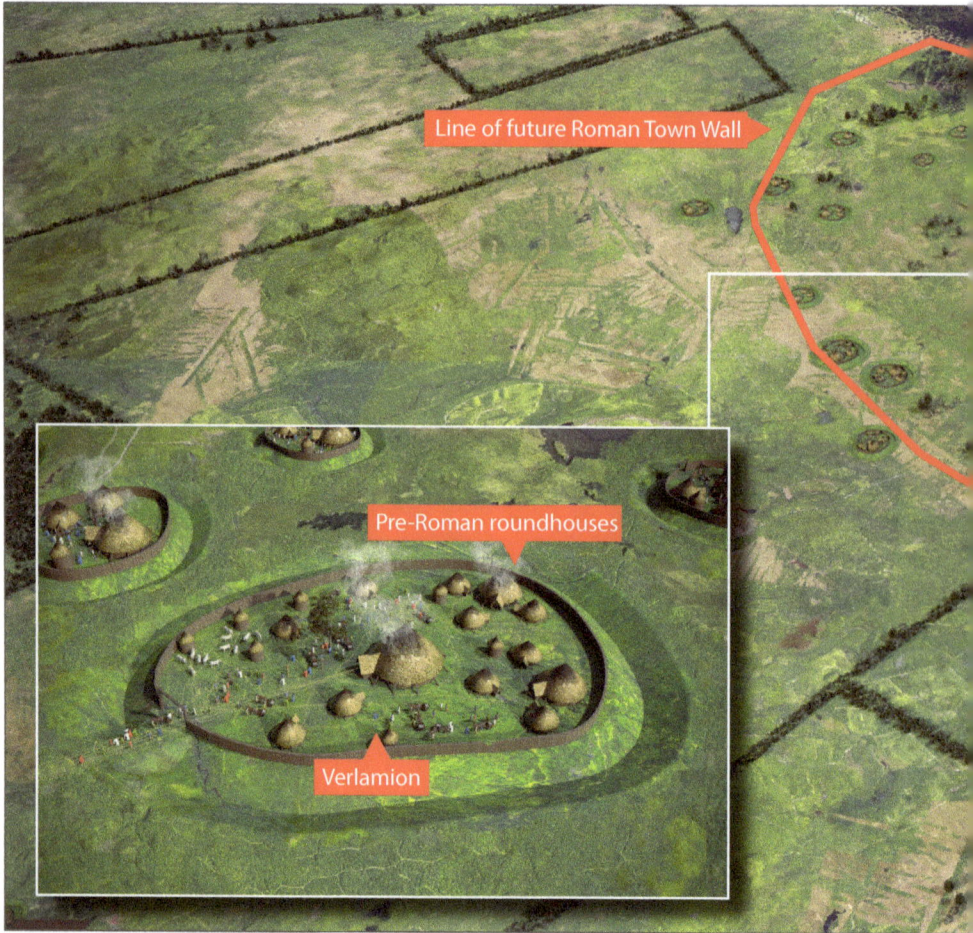

St. Albans, looking north, 30 CE.

St. Albans 30 CE

Before the Roman invasion, the area where St. Albans now stands was part of the territory of the *Catuvellauni*[1] tribe. Around 30 CE the *Catuvellauni* had allied with the eastern *Trinovante* tribe. They were ruled by *King Cunobelin (based near present day Colchester)*. Across this area were settlements the Romans called *oppida*[2]. One of these called *'Verlamion'*[3] was located on the edge of present day St. Albans. At that time there were many enclosures surrounding *Catuvellauni* homesteads. The most important are thought to have been located where the present day Verulamium Museum stands. The area was a hive of activity, with weaving, pottery and metal working.

1. Catuvellauni is thought to mean 'excellent fighters'.
2. Oppidum, loosely translated as 'town' in Latin, a native Briton fortified settlement.
3. Verlamion, which meant 'the settlement above the marsh'.

Find out more
Most of the Catuvellauni enclosures and buildings have been lost to time, although some have been discovered by archaeologists.
The Verulamium Museum has Iron Age (pre-Roman) artefacts found in the area on display.
The outline of the 4th century Roman wall (red line) is shown on the main image and the map to help you compare the past and present.

N
Marsh
Wooden causeway
Potters
River Ver
Weavers
Metal workers

N
Verlamion
Line of future Roman Town Wall
Verulamium Park
The Hypocaust
Praewood Farm
Wood

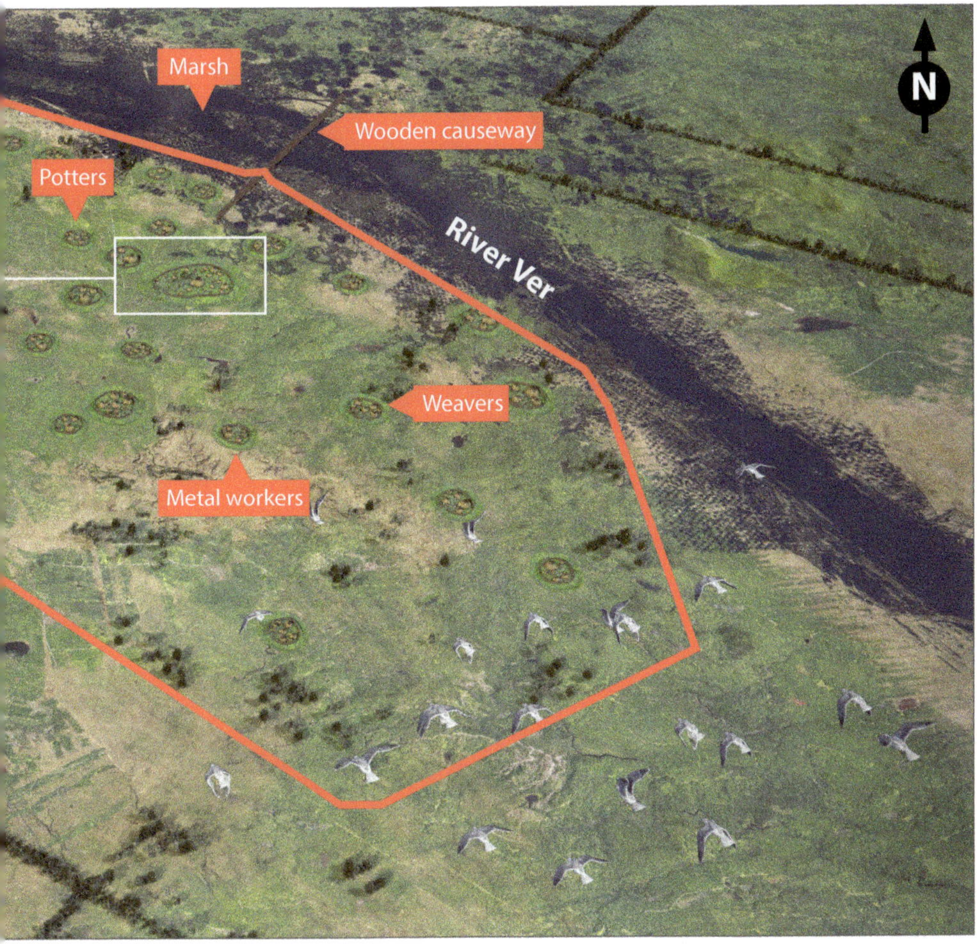

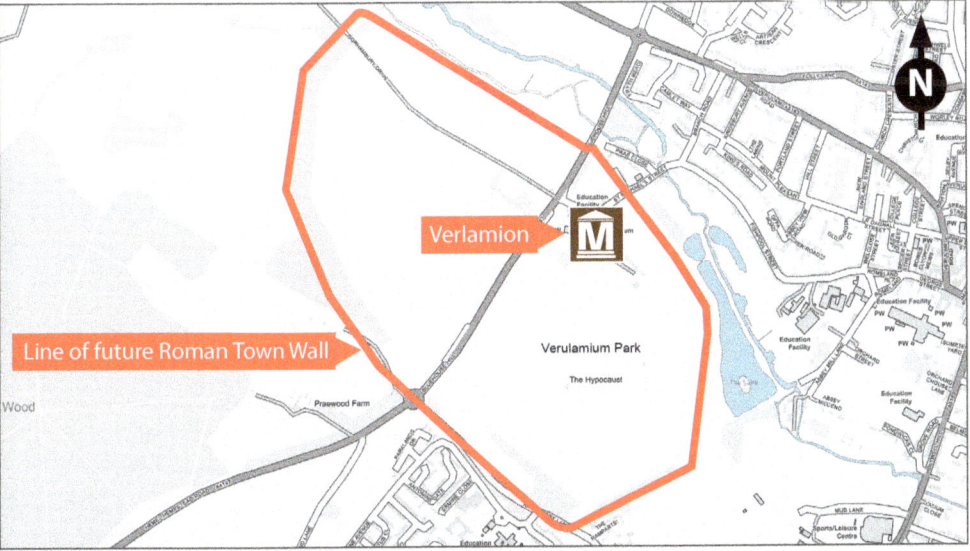

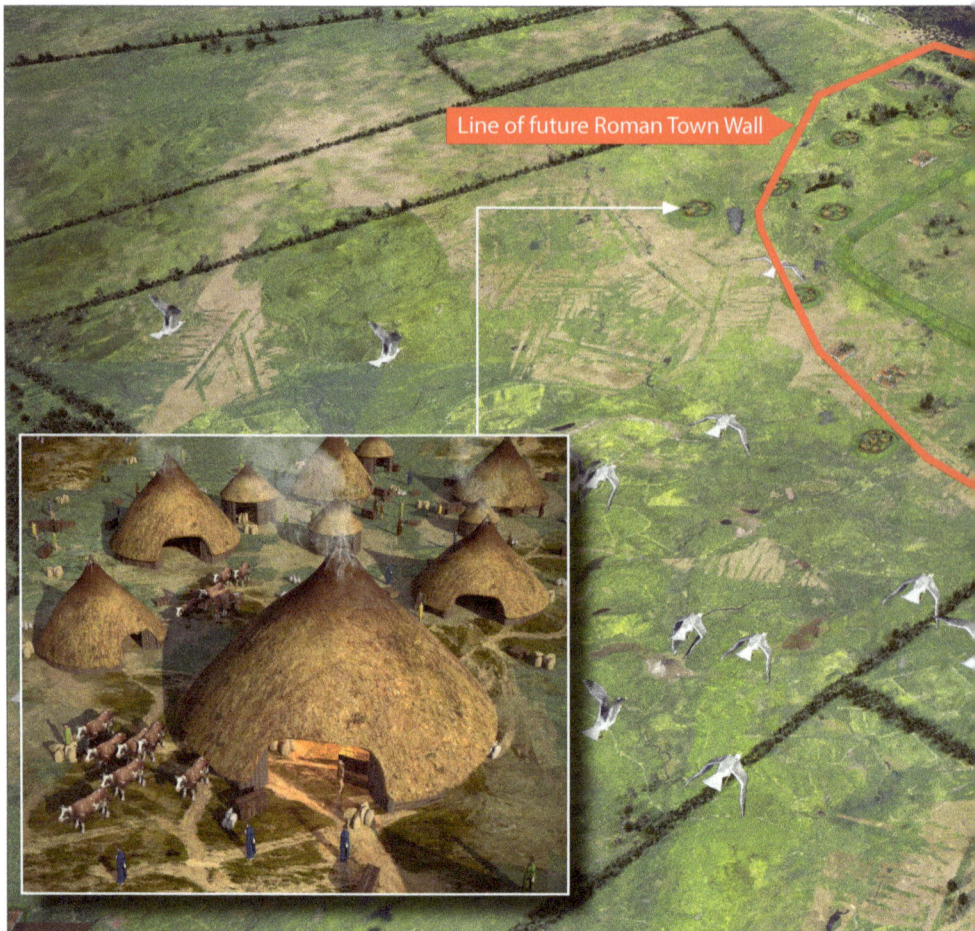

St. Albans, looking north, 50 CE. The inset shows a close-up view of a roundhouse.

St. Albans 50 CE

One might assume that when the Romans invaded in 43 CE that every tribe wanted to fight the Romans, when in fact the situation was much more complicated. It seems that the *Atrebates*[1] tribe had actually requested the Romans' assistance against the growing threat of the *Catuvellauni* and *Trinovante* tribes. Even more complicated was that the people in the present day St. Albans area were actually quietly pro-Roman. This was to have dire consequences for them around eleven years later *(see next page)*. But by 50 CE a small Roman settlement was starting to grow. *Verlamion* was given the Roman name of *Verulamium* and had become a *municipium*[2].

1. Based around the present day south-east England area.
2. A city or town which was second only to a *Colonia*[3].
3. People who lived in a *Colonia*, such as the one at Colchester, were citizens of Rome, and were often ex-soldiers.

Find out more

Typically when the Romans occupied a new area they created a marching camp called a Castra. There is debate if or where such a castra might have been located. But by 50 CE there was most probably just a collection of buildings centred around the original centre of Verlamion (see main image). As this was to be built over later on, there are no remains visible today.

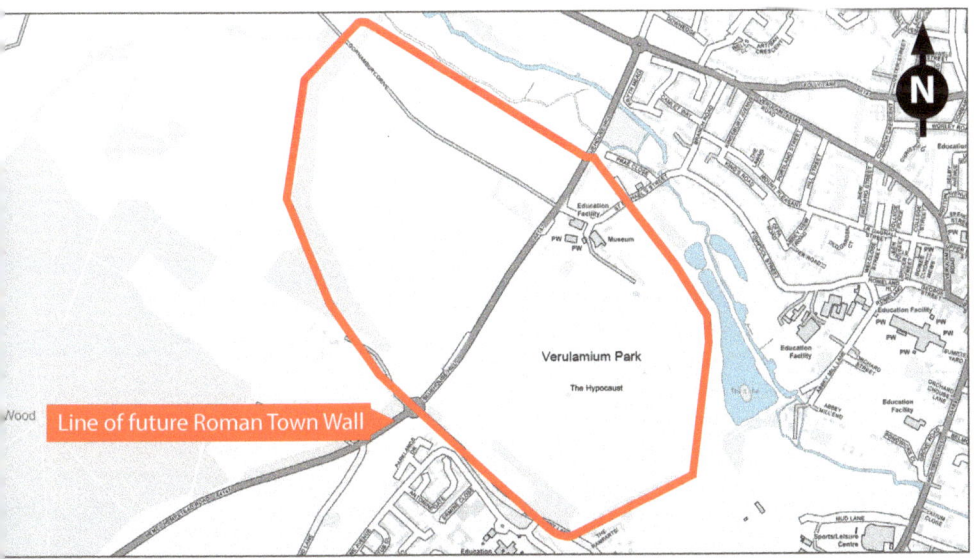

St.Albans under attack by Boudica's forces, looking north, 60-61 CE.

Boudica destroys St. Albans

In 60/61 CE the *Iceni*[1] mounted a rebellion against the occupying Roman forces. The *Iceni* led by *Queen Boudica*[2] swept south, gathering around 120,000 warriors, including people from the *Trinovantes*[3] tribe. Their first target was Colchester, which at the time had a small garrison of around 500 Roman soldiers and possibly a few thousand ex-soldiers. *Boudica* and her forces then destroyed *Londinium (London)* before marching on St. Albans. At the time St. Albans was only starting to grow and so probably did not have many buildings. It is thought the reason it was targeted was that the local tribes were pro-Roman and so *Boudica* and her forces felt justified in attacking them.

1. A tribe that ruled the area roughly covered by Norfolk.
2. There are different spellings of Boudica/Boudicca/Boadicea that have been used since Roman times.
3. A tribe that ruled the area roughly covered by Essex.

Find out more

Archaeologists have not found large amounts of evidence of the attack by Boudica and her forces, although some buildings uncovered during archaeological digs were thought to have been burnt during the attack. The blue arrows show a suggested route Boudica's forces took south from London to St. Albans and north onto Watling Street, where her final battle took place.

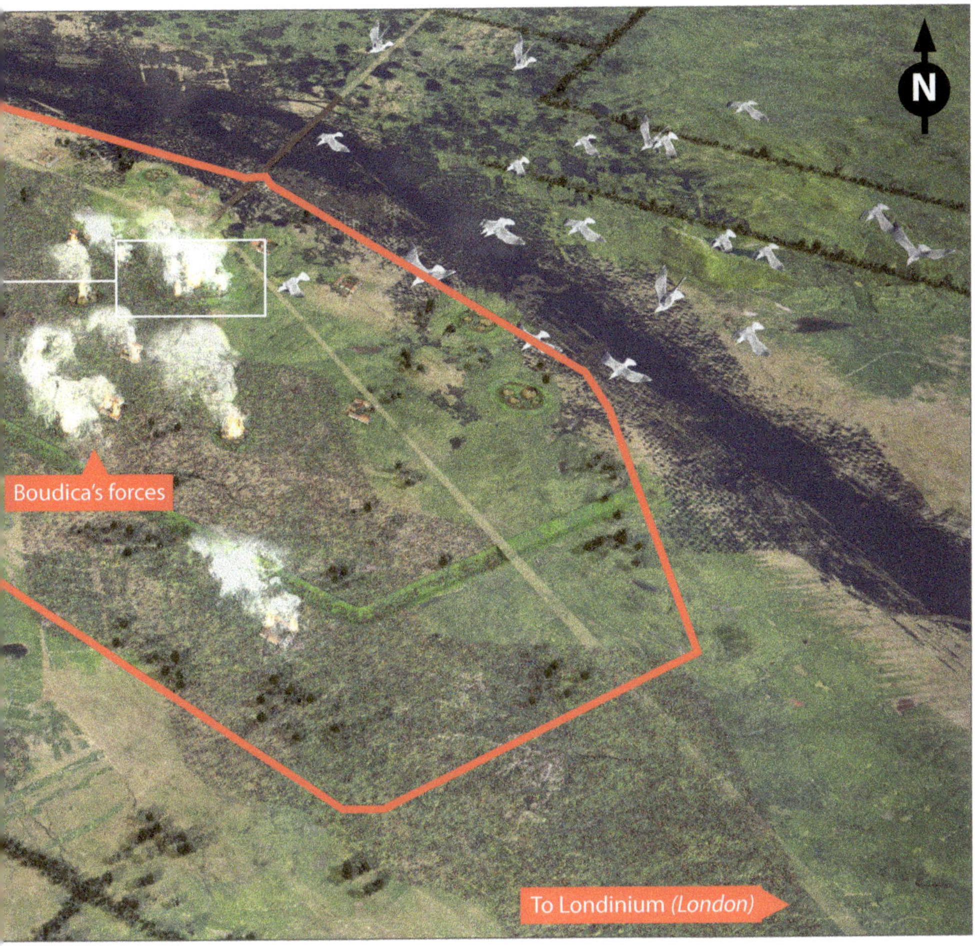

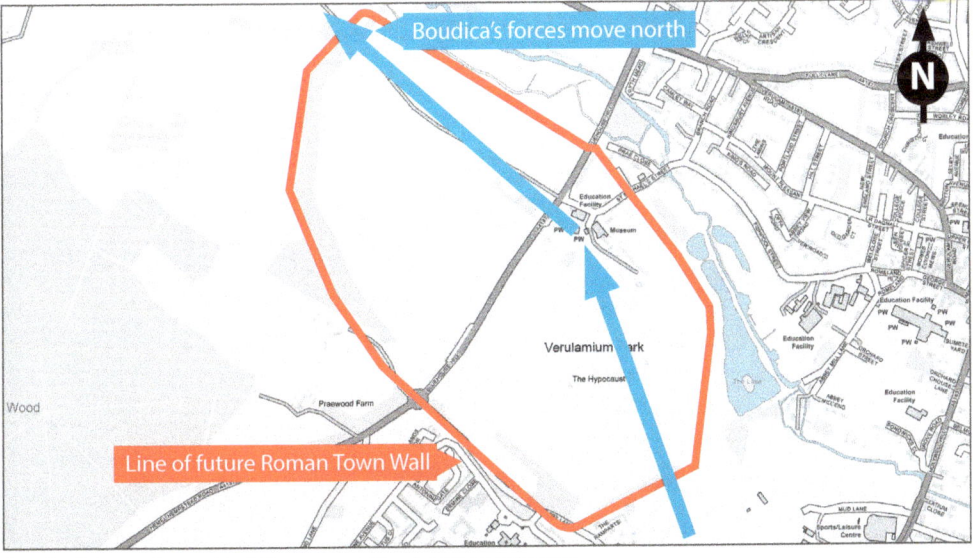

St. Albans looking north, 150 CE.

St. Albans 150 CE

After the devastating attack by *Boudica*, St Albans took many years to recover and may well never have done so if *Londinium* (London) had not become Britain's new capital city[1]. Being so close to *Londinium*, the huge amount of trade allowed *Verulamium* (St. Albans) to flourish. The whole town was angled to connect with the Romans' extensive road network. By this time a defensive ditch[2] had been built, although not a defensive wall, and large public buildings such as the Forum and Basilica had been built. The citizens of *Verulamium* would have had access to large public baths, markets, temples and much more. Around 155 CE another massive fire burnt a large section of the town, although this one was not the result of an attack, but an accident.

1. Colonia Victricensis (Colchester) was Britain's first capital city.
2. This ditch was known as 'The Fosse' and provided a set of basic defences for Verulamium.

Find out more

The layout of Verulamium can be seen to be tilted to fit the road network which converges at St. Albans.

A couple of present day roads follow the route of the Roman roads (see map).

The theatre dating from around 140 CE and surrounding buildings can be seen, as shown on the map.

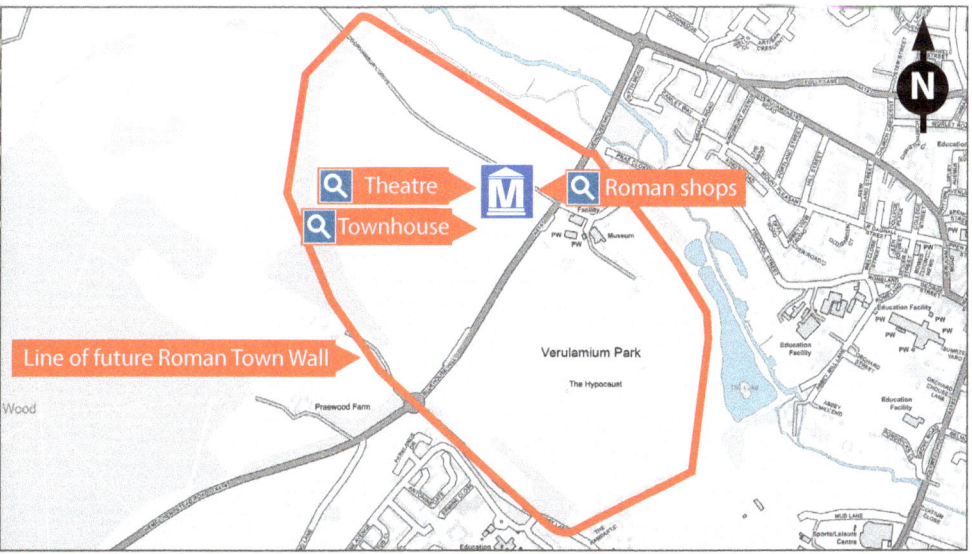

St. Albans looking north, 270 CE.

St. Albans 270 CE

By this time the Roman Empire was gradually starting to crumble. *Dio Cassius (a Roman historian)* commented that the empire went *"from a kingdom of gold to one of rust and iron"*. As part of this upheaval the *Emperor Septimius Severus* actually ruled the whole empire for a few years from York while fighting the northern tribes. At that time Britain was split into two areas: *Britannia Superior (south)* and *Britannia Inferior (north)* with York *(Eboracum)* governing the north. Rather than any dramatic events, such as the fire of 155 CE, St. Albans started a gradual decline, with many of the rich villa owners starting to run into financial difficulties.
But public building works continued, such as the Town Wall, monumental arches and adding a canal. The Town Wall was not thought to be for defensive reasons, but rather for visual impact. Over the following centuries *Verulamium* declined and the new city of St. Albans was formed to the east.

Find out more

*Remains of the Roman Town Wall can be seen, as shown on the map along with the part of the Roman Theatre.
Note the amphitheatre is conjectural, as it has not been located, but most Roman towns had one.*

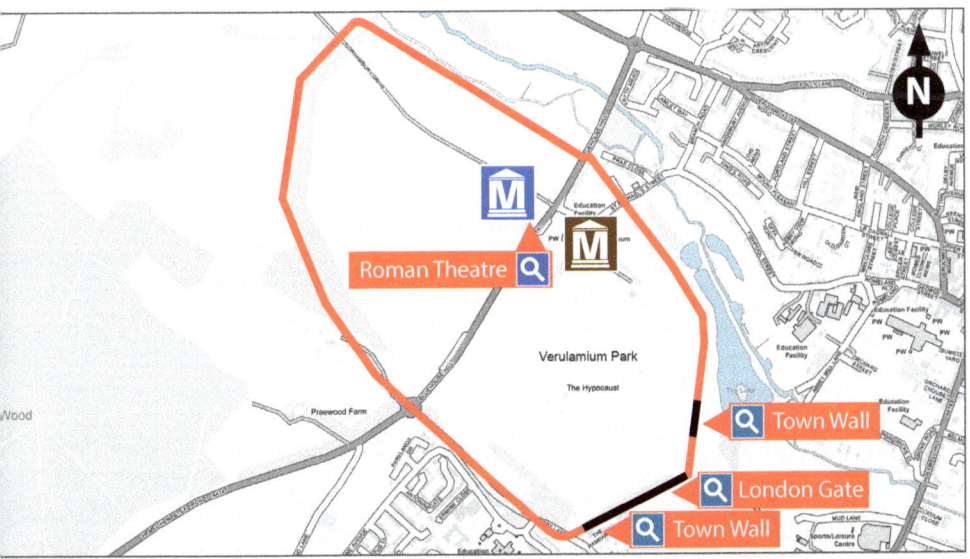

14. The Roman Theatre

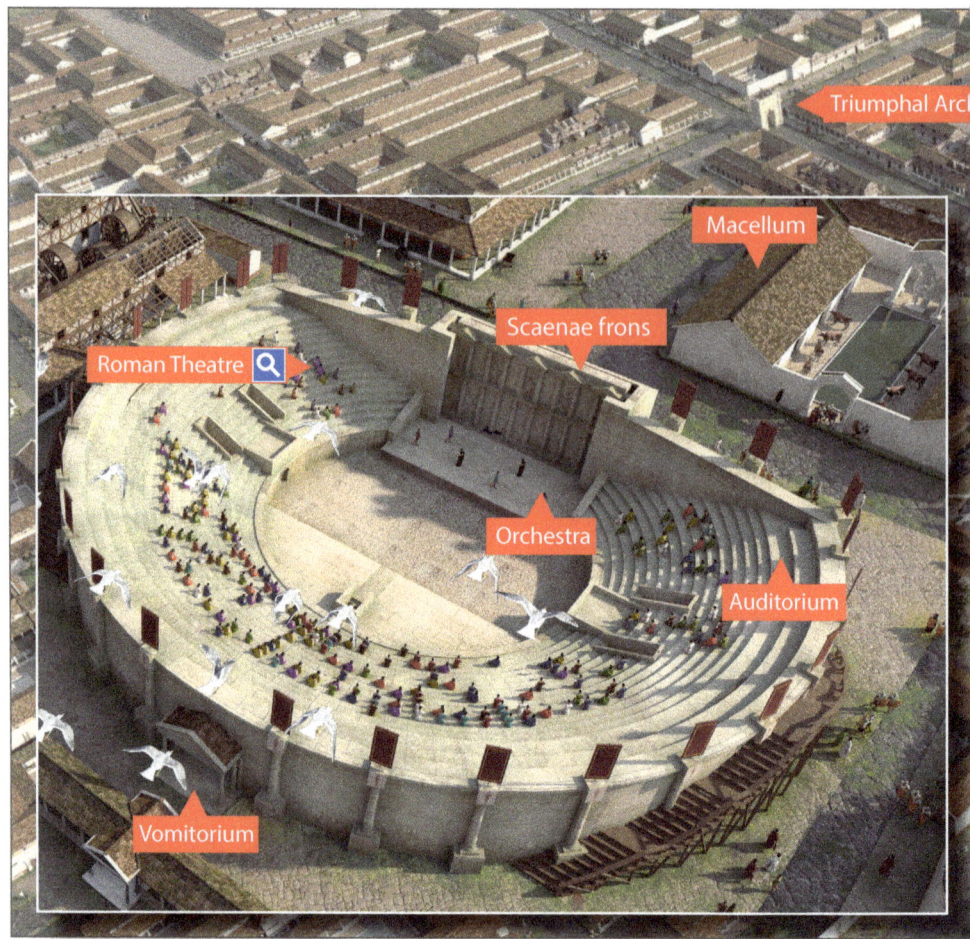

Site of the Roman Theatre, Townhouse and shops, looking north, 270 CE.

The Roman Theatre

Verulamium, as with other Roman towns, had a theatre. Pantomimes were more popular than plays, as well as comedies based on people's lives. This theatre may have also had religious events, as it was near to a temple.
It was built around 145 CE and had wooden outer stairs and wooden internal seating which eventually seated about 2000 people. The building may have stood over 16 metres *(52 feet)* tall with a large and complex stage area including the *Scaenae frons*, which was full of columns and provided a background for the actors. The audience would have entered the theatre through the *Vomitorium* and sat in the semi-circular *Auditorium*, overlooking the *Orchestra (stage)*. Next to the theatre archaeologists discovered a townhouse and shops, possibly used by metalworkers. *Verulamium* became well know for jewellery production, as many exotic materials have been found, such as gold and emerald.

Find out more
The Roman Theatre is one of the best preserved in England and along with the Roman shops and townhouse can be seen at the Roman Theatre of Verulamium Museum (blue square). A model of the Theatre and sections from the stage can also be seen at the Verulamium Museum (brown square). Also shown on this image are sites found by archaeologists including a macellum (market), triumphal arch, aqueduct, gatehouses and temples.

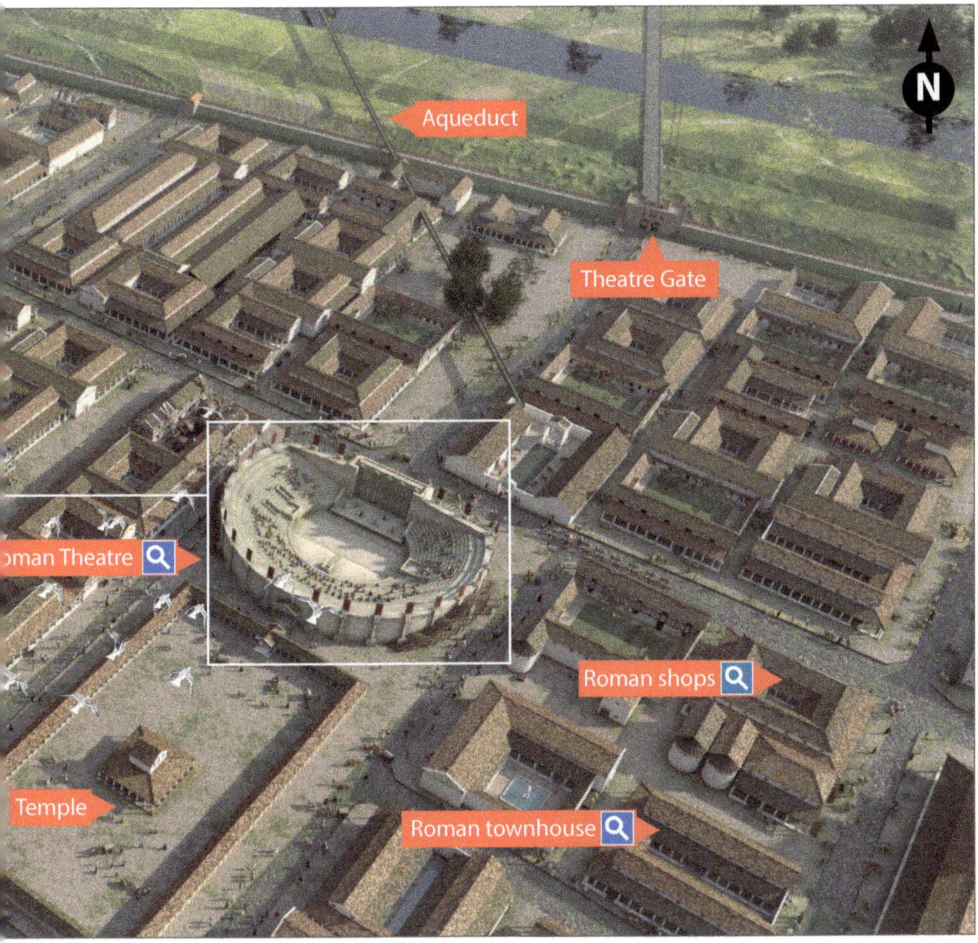

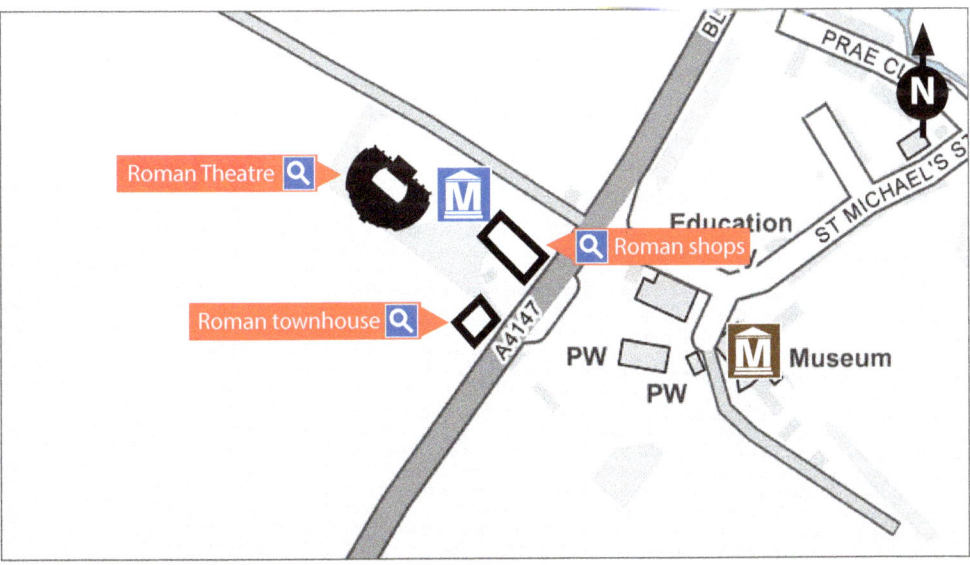

A possible view of the Floral Mosaic in 170 CE. The inset shows a close up of part of the mosaic.

The Floral Mosaic

This mosaic, known as the *Floral Mosaic*, was discovered in the same townhouse as the *Oceanus Mosaic* (see page 20) and dates from around 170 CE. The mosaic may have been located in the townhouse's *Triclinium* (dining room). Here the owner would have entertained guests, possibly wealthy merchants or politicians. Inside the *Triclinium* there would have been ornate furniture such as *Lectus tricliniaris (lounges)*, and fine foods. The Romans had heated floors, called a *hypocaust*[1] which transferred heat from a furnace under the floor, usually run by slaves. The floor was raised from the ground on small sets of columns called *pilae*. The excess heat was vented through chimneys in the walls. Less wealthy people would have had to heat their homes with open fires.

1. The word Hypocaust came originally from the Greek words Hypo (under) and caust (burnt).

Find out more

The Floral Mosaic and part of the hypocaust are on display in a custom built building inside the Verulamium Park. The wall paintings are speculative and are based on ones seen in Rome.

A view showing how much of the mosaic and hypocaust can be seen in the present day.

18. *The Shell Mosaic*

A possible interior of the house where the Shell Mosaic was located, around 150 CE.

The Shell Mosaic

The Shell Mosaic, built around 150 CE, is an uncommon design, not often seen in Britain. It may have formed part of the floor of an *apse*. An semi-circular *apse* formed part of the main hall of large Roman houses, which were sometimes used to entertain guests of the homeowners.

Roman mosaics were usually based around squares, featuring either creatures or geometric patterns, rather than the semi-circular shell[1] mosaic seen here. It is likely that the artisans who made up the mosaic offered their services to the town, rich villa owners and clients as far away as Colchester.

1. Shell designs were associated with Venus, the goddess of love and beauty. Around the edge of the shell are waves, which feature in many Venus mosaics found in Roman Britain.

Find out more

The Shell Mosaic, which has survived the centuries remarkably well, is on display at the Verulamium Museum. The above image shows a suggested location for the Shell Mosaic, to help visualise how it may have looked. The wall paintings are speculative and are based on ones seen in Rome.

The Romans were great admirers of roses and even had special festivals called Rosalia.

A view showing how much of the mosaic can be seen in the present day.

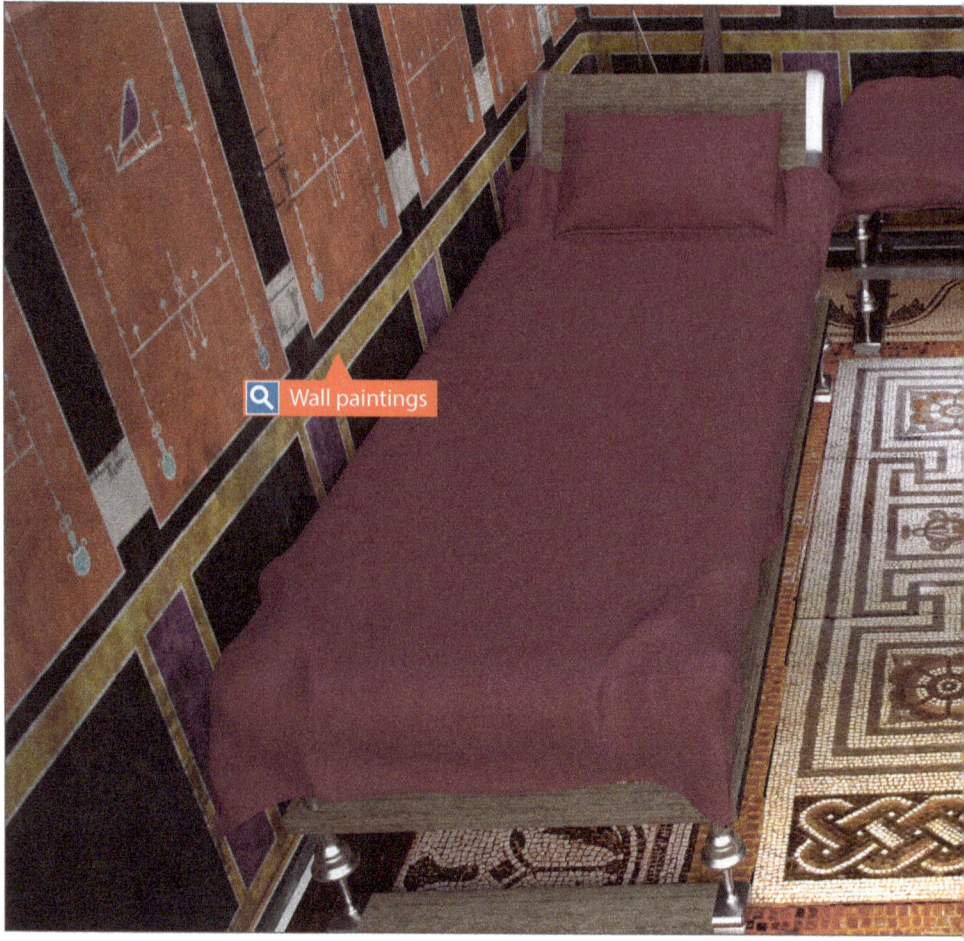

Possible interior of the house which housed the Oceanus Mosaic, around 165 CE.

The Oceanus Mosaic

Many of the wealthy houses in Roman Britain had elaborate mosaics on the floors. Mosaics are made up of hundreds of small squares of coloured tiles called *tesserae*.

These tesserae were laid into a flat surface covered with mortar, which made them long-lasting and allowed for complex designs. One such design was built around 160 CE and depicts either *Oceanus*[1] or *Cernunnos*[2] with flowers and canthari[3] around the edges. There is some debate about which god the mosaic actually represents, as if it is *Oceanus* then typically he would be surrounded by sea creatures.

1. Oceanus was originally from Greek mythology and had crab claws on his head, which may be shown on the mosaic.
2. Cernunnos is interpreted by some scholars as the god of nature, and was a fusion of Celtic and Roman mythology.
3. A large two-handled drinking vessel or cup.

Find out more

The Oceanus Mosaic is on display in excellent condition at the Verulamium Museum. Note that the outer mosaic and interior are speculative, although the wall paintings are based on ones displayed at the Verulamium museum. Archaeologists found large sections of wall paintings, painted onto plaster at Verulamium, that centuries before had collapsed due to water damage when the houses fell apart after the fall of the Roman Empire.

A view showing how much of the mosaic and wall paintings can be seen in the present day.

A possible view of the Venus Figurine around 220 CE.

The Venus Figurine

Although this figurine is known as the *Venus Figurine*, it is thought that it actually depicts *Persephone*. She was a mythological figure who was abducted by the god *Hades* and became the goddess of the Underworld.
Persephone represented spring and was associated with the growth of crops, as shown on this figurine with her holding a pomegranate. Typically statues or figurines depicting the goddess *Venus* usually show her naked, while this figurine is partially clothed, leading archaeologists to believe it depicts *Persephone*. The bronze figurine was probably used in a wealthy townhouse's private *lararium*[1] and possibly dates from around 220 CE.

1. A shrine inside a house was known as a lararium, and often contained a couple of figurines, such as the Venus figurine. The family would pray to the gods and leave offerings such as food and drink.

Find out more

The Venus Figurine is on display at the Verulamium Museum. The main image suggests how it might have looked when new, while the image on the right shows how it looks in the present day.

A view showing how much of the figurine can be seen in the present day.

A possible view of amphorae in a Verulamium shop, around 140 CE.

Roman amphorae

Amphorae were produced in vast quantities throughout the Roman Empire. They were used for transporting mostly liquid food and drink products, such as fish sauces, olive oil and wines. Most had pointed ends, which at first may seem like a design flaw. In fact, they were a highly effective design, typically used on ships, where their design allowed them to be packed tightly together, protecting their contents. *Amphorae*, like many other designs used by the Romans, were not invented by them. Archaeologists have found evidence of their use in the seas of Syria around 1,500 BCE. Some of the amphorae on display in the Verulamium Museum originated from southern Spain and stored olive oil, while others stored a rather potent fermented fish sauce called *garum*. Other *amphorae* were used to transport dates grown in *Roman Judea (present day Palestine)*, around 3,596 km *(2,234 miles)* from *Verulamium*.

Find out more
There are fine examples of Roman amphorae on display at the Verulamium Museum. Some of them could hold up to 100 litres (22 gallons). The spikes at the base of the amphorae were used during transport and to help with pouring out liquids. The amphorae would have had stoppers, but these typically were made of less durable materials and so did not survive to the present day.

Roman amphorae

Roman amphorae
Museum
Education Facility
Education Facility
Verulamium Park
BLUEHOUSE HILL
PRAE CLOSE
ST MICHAEL'S STREET
KING'S ROAD
THE LAWNS
MOUNT PLEASANT
FISHPOOL STREET
OFFA ROAD
ABBEY VIEW ROAD
N

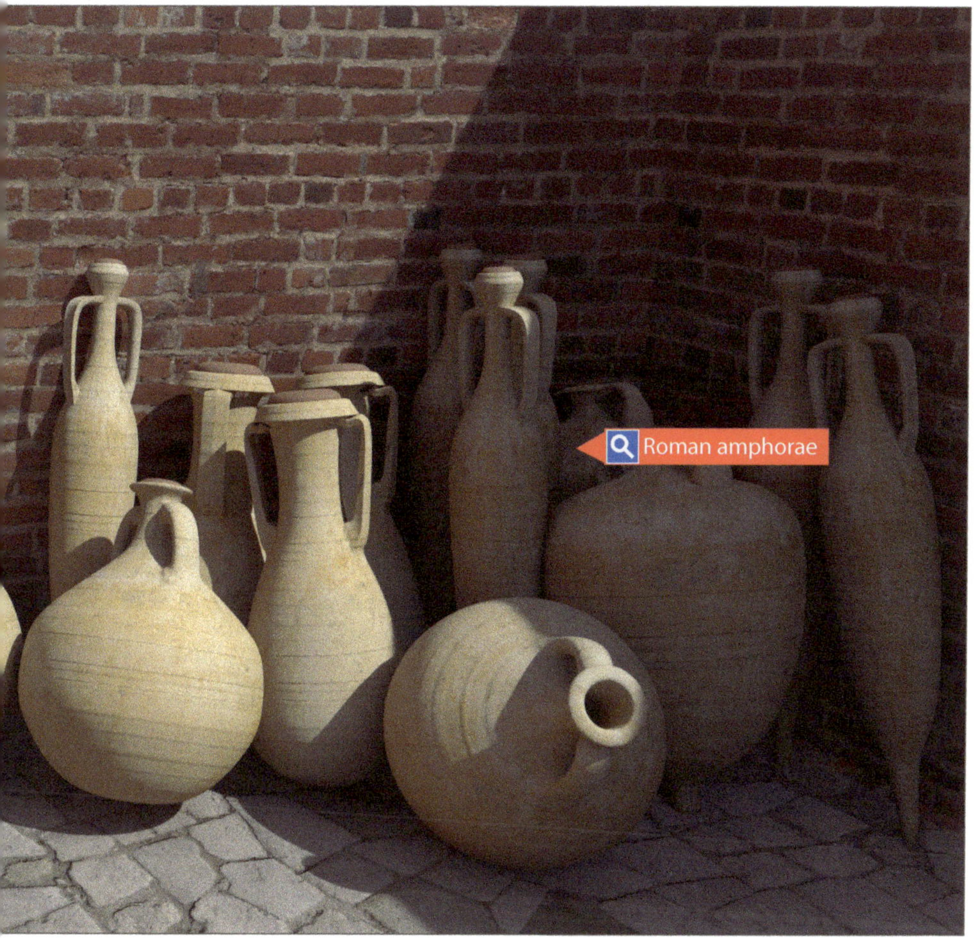

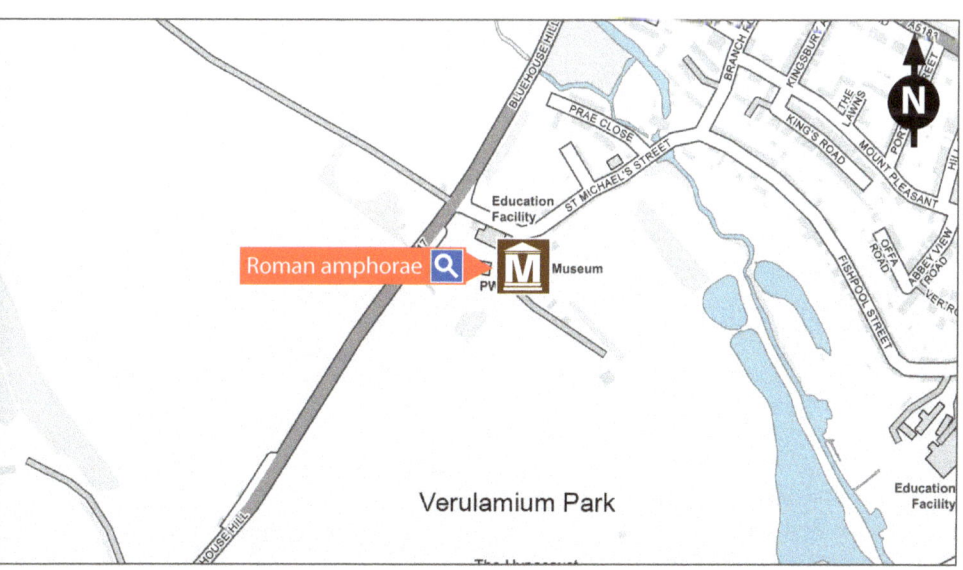

26. The Town Wall

The Town Wall, looking north, 270 CE.

The Town Wall

Around 265 CE construction was completed on the Town Wall, which was made of stone. It was about 5 metres *(16.4 feet)* high and possibly 2.4 metres *(7.8 feet)* thick and 3.6 kilometres *(2.2 miles)* long. Outside was a defensive ditch for further protection. Around the wall there were at least five gatehouses and many towers guarded by centurions, legionaries and auxiliaries. The main image also shows how the Town Wall was a continuous circuit, so that troops could move to any part rapidly. At the end of most streets or corners there were guard-towers which would be used as observation posts. Combined with the defensive ditch, the Town Wall made the town much easier to defend. After the Roman period the walls were slowly broken up and reused as building materials, until only two sections in the Verulamium Park survived.

Find out more

Most of the Roman Town Wall no longer survives except for two well-preserved sections (shown in black on the map). The lower section includes the foundations of the London Gate. Both sections can be seen inside the Verulamium Park.

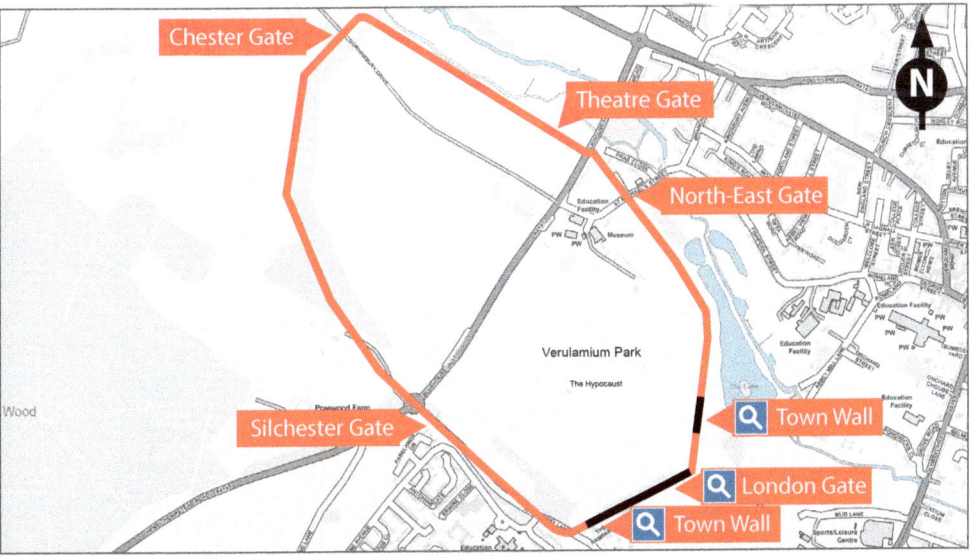

The site of the Basilica and Forum, looking north, 270 CE.

The Basilica and Forum

The *Basilica* was the commercial and administrative heart of *Verulamium*, and was where deals were made and laws practised. The Romans had a highly sophisticated legal system which underpins civil law practised in modern times. Large statues would have dominated the *Forum (public square)* where the population of the local area could meet. Surrounding the *Forum* were various offices for local administrators and merchants. There would probably also have been market stalls selling food and household items sourced from all over the Roman Empire. Some of the merchants who traded here became very rich and built large villas in the surrounding countryside. The *Basilica* and *Forum* are thought to be have been first built around 78 CE, although they were destroyed in the 155 CE fire. They were rebuilt around 175 CE, although they differed slightly from the originals, with the Forum gaining a new temple.

Find out more

Most of the Basilica and Forum no longer survives, although parts of its foundations are marked in the Verulamium Museum carpark. Part of an inscription marking one of the entrances to the Basilica is also displayed inside the museum. Also shown on this image are sites found by archaeologists including a Bathhouse, Triumphal Arch, gatehouses and temples.

The amphitheatre is speculative, but most Roman towns had one.

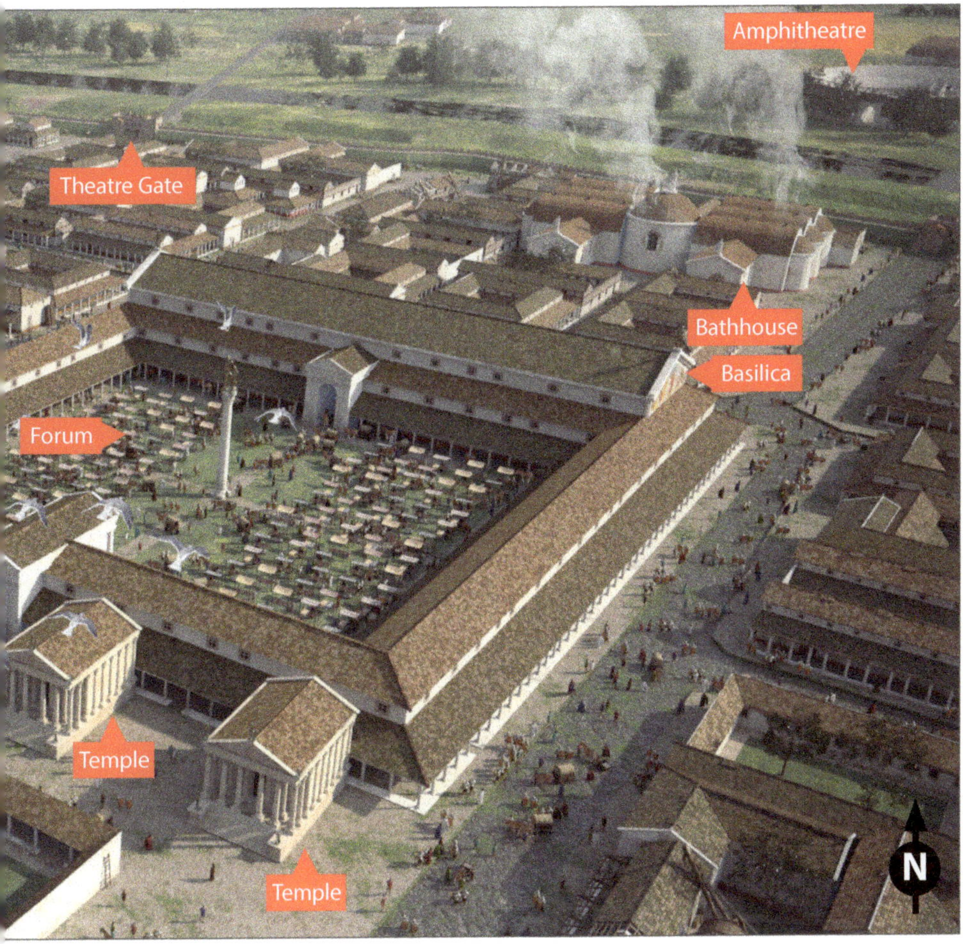

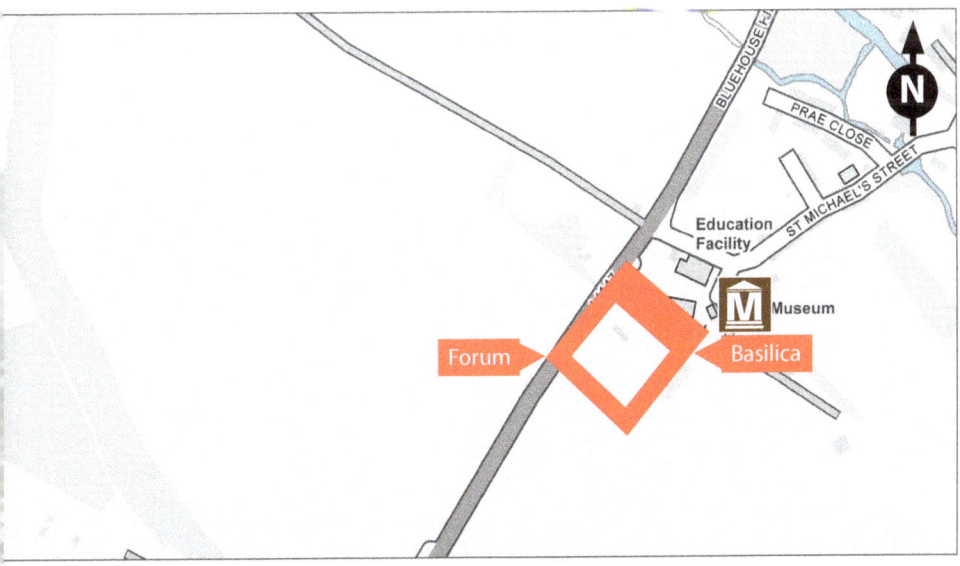

The Temple of Cybele, looking north, 200 CE.

The Temple of Cybele

Around 140 CE a temple, called the *Triangle Temple*[1] by archaeologists, was built near to the London Gate (see page 28). It was probably dedicated to the *'Mother-Goddess Cybele or Magna Mater*[2], as she was known by the Romans. Archaeologists found remains of burnt pine-cones at the site of the temple, not native to Britain, which may have been used in religious ceremonies. *Cybele* was first worshipped around 600 BCE in the area which is now present day Turkey. Originally a Greek goddess, over the centuries she became incorporated in Roman religion.

She was also seen as a protector of towns and cities, and so was worshipped to protect *Verulamium*.

1. The site was called the 'Triangle Temple' by archaeologists due to its unusual design, which had to fit into the street plan near to the London Gate.
2. Magna Mater, roughly translates as Great Mother.

Find out more

There are no visible remains of the Temple of Cybele, which was found in the Verulamium Park.
The image above also shows a Triumphal Arch found by archaeologists and cattle being taken to market along the main road into the town. Archaeologists have found evidence of what food was eaten in Verulamium, including cattle bones.

N
Triumphal Arch

Education
Facility
PW
PW
Museum
N
Verulamium Park
The Hypocaust
Temple of Cybele
Praewood Farm
BLUEHOUSE HILL
A4147

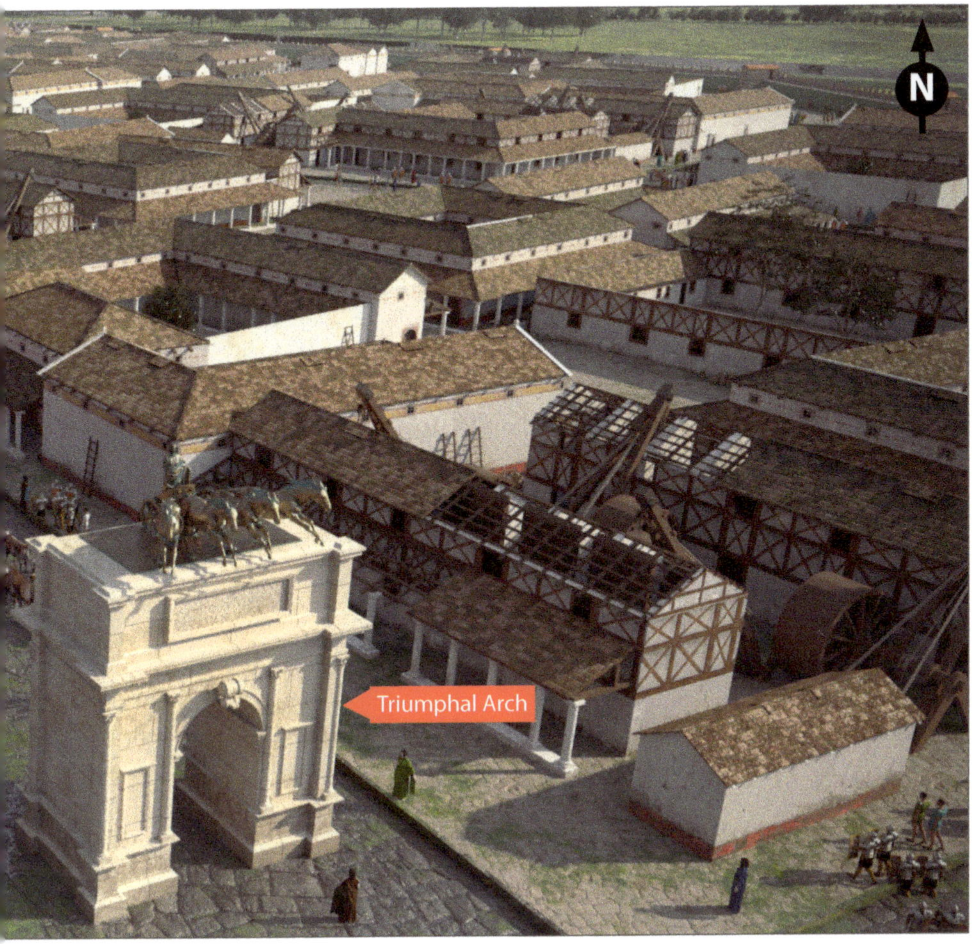

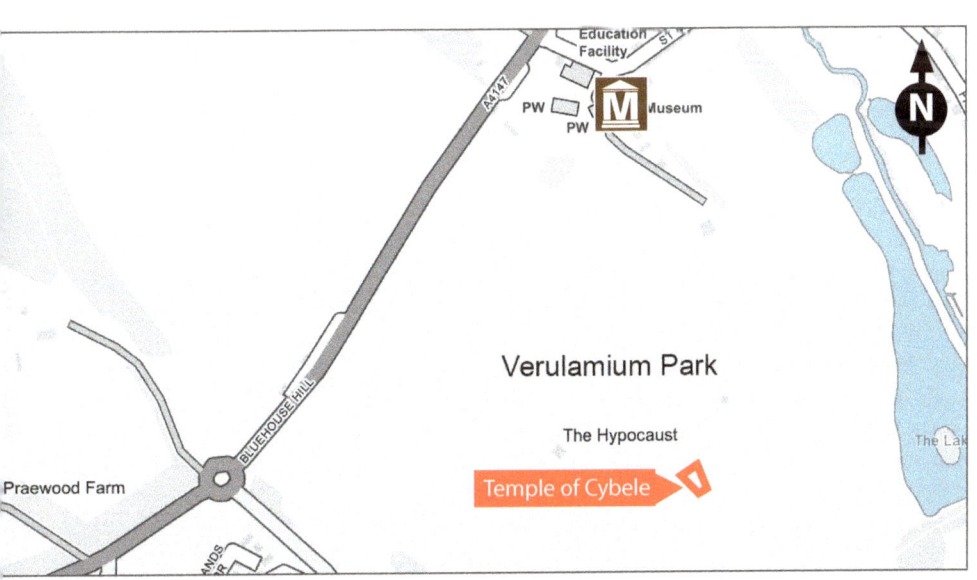

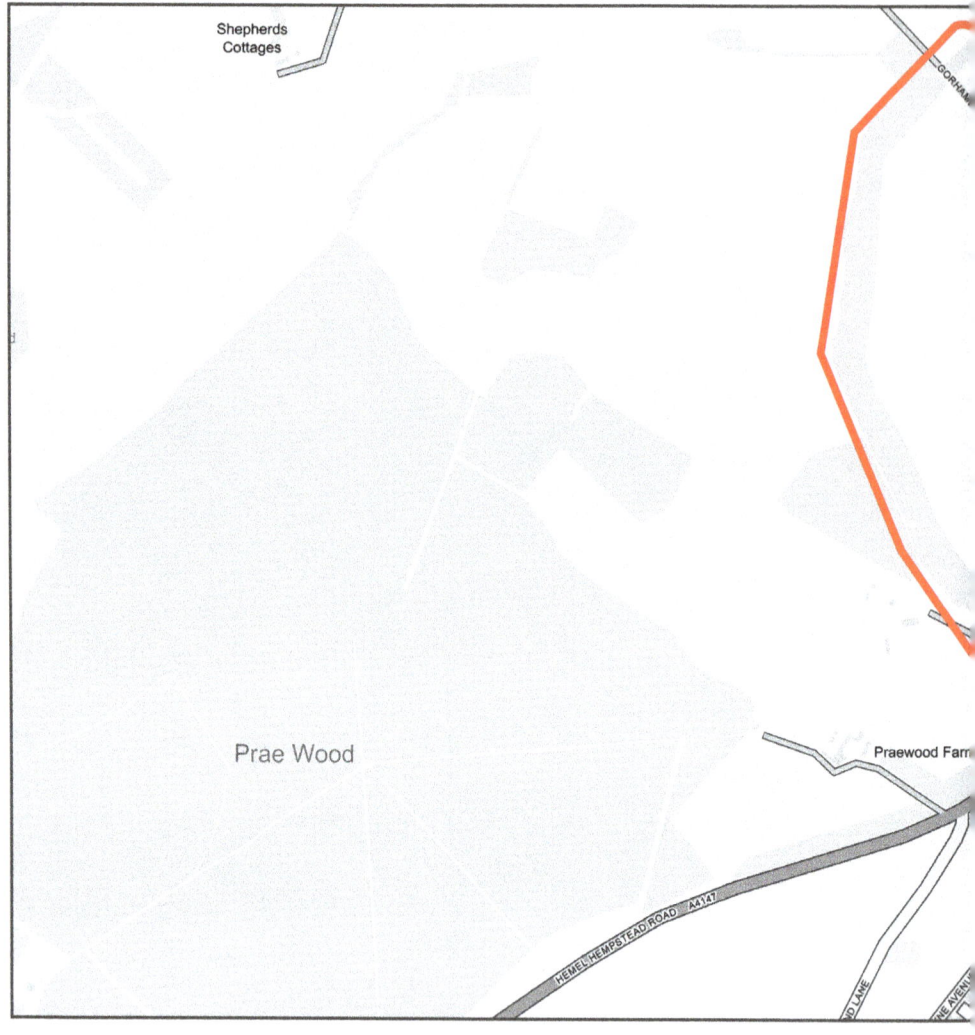

Roman St. Albans today

Verulamium lies to the west of the present day St. Albans city centre. Most of the Roman sites lie inside the Verulamium Park, which has parking facilities. The Roman Theatre of Verulamium site lies just a few minutes from the Verulamium Museum.

The red lines show where the original Roman walls were and the black lines show where partial Roman walls can still be seen. The sites shown on this map are also explored in more detail in the main part of this book, as well as showing where the main museums in St. Albans are which feature Roman artefacts. All the exterior images of face north, so that you can compare the past with the present day maps.

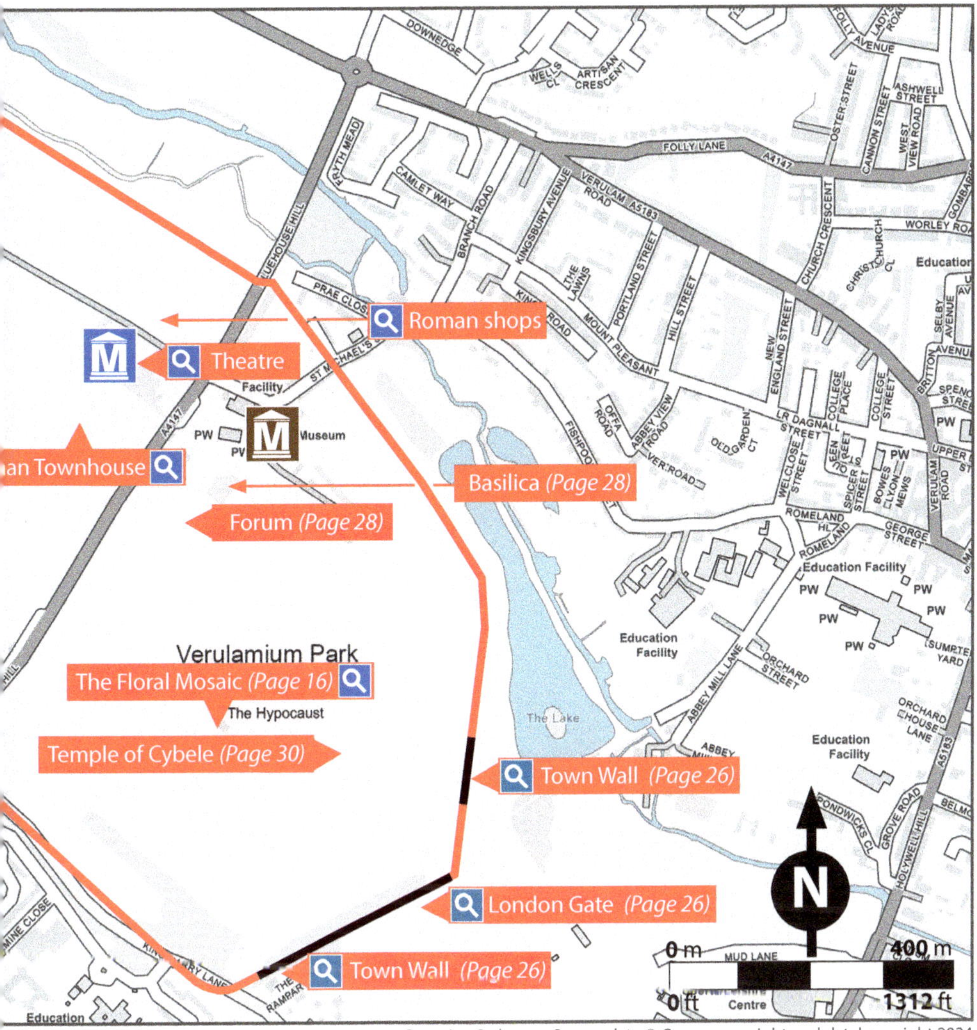

Contains Ordnance Survey data © Crown copyright and database right 2024

Symbols used on this map

— Outlines of Roman walls *(still visible)*

— Outlines of Roman walls *(no longer visible)*

 Theatre
Roman points of interest *(still visible)*

 Temple
Roman points of interest *(no longer visible)*

 Roman Theatre of Verulamium *(Page 14)*

Verulamium Museum
Displaying multiple artefacts including:
The Shell Mosaic (P 18)
The Oceanus Mosaic (P 20)
The Venus Figurine (P 22)
Roman amphorae (P 24)

First published March 2024
ISBN 978-1-7391254-6-2 *(Paperback)*
First Edition

Designed and published by JC3DVIS
www.jc3dvis.co.uk
Book design © 2024 Joseph Chittenden

All the images in this guide were produced by JC3DVIS.
Contains Ordnance Survey data © Crown copyright and database right 2024

The moral right of the copyright holder has been asserted.

All rights reserved. No part of this publication may be reproduced, distributed or transmitted in any form or by any means, including photocopying, recording, or other electronic or mechanical methods, without the prior written permission of the publisher.

With special thanks to:
Jane Chittenden

Legal disclaimer
Neither the author nor the publisher shall be held liable or responsible to any person or entity with respect to any loss or incidental or consequential damages caused, or alleged to have been caused, directly or indirectly, by the information contained herein.

The computer generated model of Roman St Albans is based on archaeological data after Rosalind Niblett and Professor Sheppard Frere.

www.ingramcontent.com/pod-product-compliance
Lightning Source LLC
Chambersburg PA
CBHW042123100526
44587CB00025B/4161